A Crabtree Branches Book

Improving Your Social Skills

HOW TO DEAL WITH A BULLY

VICKY BUREAU

Crabtree Publishing
crabtreebooks.com

School-to-Home Support for Caregivers and Teachers

This high-interest book is designed to motivate striving students with engaging topics while building fluency, vocabulary, and an interest in reading. Here are a few questions and activities to help the reader build upon his or her comprehension skills.

Before Reading:

- *What do I think this book is about?*
- *What do I know about this topic?*
- *What do I want to learn about this topic?*
- *Why am I reading this book?*

During Reading:

- *I wonder why...*
- *I'm curious to know...*
- *How is this like something I already know?*
- *What have I learned so far?*

After Reading:

- *What was the author trying to teach me?*
- *What are some details?*
- *How did the photographs and captions help me understand more?*
- *Read the book again and look for the vocabulary words.*
- *What questions do I still have?*

Extension Activities:

- *What was your favorite part of the book? Write a paragraph on it.*
- *Draw a picture of your favorite thing you learned from the book.*

TABLE OF CONTENTS

FEELING SAD OR SCARED?

Have you ever felt scared or sad at school because of something someone else said or did? Did it continue to happen?

Was someone in your school purposely making you feel bad? Did they continue to do it over and over again?

DID YOU KNOW?

Bullying impacts one in five students in the United States and one in seven in Canada.

ARE YOU BEING BULLIED?

Unfortunately, sometimes people can be **unkind** to each other. Students can pick on each other, call them names, and even hurt them physically.

When someone is regularly unkind to you, hurts you on **purpose** for no reason, and makes you feel powerless to stop it, you are being bullied.

BULLYING vs BEING UNKIND

Bullying is a term used to describe a situation where someone is hurt, scared, or embarrassed by another person's words or actions. It happens more than once, and victims feel like they cannot stop it. Bullying is meanness that happens often and on purpose.

It's important to know and understand the difference between bullying and being unkind.

Kindness means someone goes out of their way to make people feel good.

Bullying means someone goes out of their way to make people feel bad.

DID YOU KNOW?

There are four types of bullying: verbal, social, physical, and cyber.

CHECKPOINT: WHAT WOULD YOU DO?

Billy picks on you every morning. Yesterday he told you that your hair looked stupid. Today, he whispered about you in class and told everyone you smell bad. At recess, he tripped you while you were trying to play soccer with Alley.

You like to play soccer with Alley and Tommy at recess. Today, Alley decided to color with Tommy instead of playing soccer. They didn't invite you to color with them, which made you feel sad.

Who was the bully?

Who was being unkind?

PATTERN

When it comes to bullying, there are four Ps to consider: **Pattern**, **Power**, Purpose, and **Provoked**.

Let's talk about the first P: Pattern.

The word pattern describes something that repeats, or happens more than once. If you have cereal every day before school, you've created a pattern of eating breakfast.

Similarly, if someone is mean to you and does it every day, every other day, or even a few days a week, they have created a pattern of mistreatment towards you. When a pattern of mistreatment happens, it could be bullying.

POWER

Now let's talk about the second P: Power.

The word power describes a feeling someone has when they feel like they can control what's going on around them. If you study hard, you have the power to get good grades.

Similarly, if someone is able to control you or your feelings, they may have power over you. When someone seems more powerful than you, it can make you feel scared or sad. Even worse, you probably feel like you cannot stop it. When you feel powerless, it could be bullying.

DID YOU KNOW?

Grades can be negatively impacted by bullying.

PURPOSE

Now let's talk about the third P: Purpose.

The word purpose describes the reason why something is said or done. You may make your bed, fold your clothes, and put away your toys with the purpose of cleaning your room.

Similarly, if someone is being mean to you because they want to hurt you, they are being unkind on purpose. If someone is hurtful on purpose, it can make you feel afraid or unsafe. When someone scares you on purpose, it could be bullying.

MERRY
MAS

PROVOKE

Now let's talk about the fourth, and last, P: Provoked.

The word provoke describes something that happens as a response to an action. If you pet a cat gently, you may get her to purr. If you pull her tail, you may provoke her to bite.

Similarly, if you are unkind to someone, you may be provoking them to be unkind to you. But if you have not been unkind and they continue to be mean to you without being provoked, it could be considered bullying.

CHECKPOINT: WHAT WOULD YOU DO?

Billy makes fun of you every day. It makes you feel embarrassed. At lunch, he sometimes pushes you out of the way and cuts in front of you in line. You know it is not an accident because it happens a lot and he never says sorry. You don't push Billy back because he is bigger than you and you're worried he will hurt you even more.

Is Billy bullying you or is he being unkind? What is the difference between the two? Can you spot the four Ps?

WHY DO KIDS BULLY?

Now that we know what a bully is, let's talk about why kids become bullies. Sometimes people can be mean because they are angry. Sometimes they think they are being funny.

Believe it or not, many kids who become bullies were once a victim of bullying themselves. When this happens, it is called a **cycle of bullying**. Maybe the bully is lonely or is trying to fit in. Maybe the bully is bored or thinks it's funny. Maybe the bully feels powerless at home.

No matter what the reason is for bullying, it is never okay to do it.

DID YOU KNOW?

Many cases of bullying go unreported because the victim is afraid it will make the situation worse.

WHAT CAN YOU DO?

Your school is full of people who care about you and want you to feel safe. You can talk to your teacher about bullying. Your teacher may talk to the student to help make things better.

You should also talk to your school counselor. Your **school counselor** wants to help you feel safe. He or she will talk to the bully and help them understand how you feel, explain why bullying is wrong, and will create a plan to make it stop.

HOW CAN YOU HELP YOURSELF?

If you think you're being bullied, you can help yourself by telling an adult at school. All of the people that work at your school want you to feel happy and safe. From your principal to your bus driver, a trusted adult will know how to help make the bullying go away.

Sometimes it's hard to talk to an adult. You may feel shy or embarrassed. You can also talk to your parents if you think you are being bullied. The people who take care of you at home will work with the grown-ups at your school to make sure the bullying problem has been addressed.

HOW CAN YOU HELP OTHERS?

DID YOU KNOW?

More than half of bullying cases stop when an upstander intervenes.

If you think someone else is being bullied, you can help them, too!

When you see something and say something, you become an **upstander**. An upstander is someone who stands up to bullying by sticking up for the victim. Just like a bully goes out of their way to do the wrong thing, an upstander goes out of their way to do the right thing.

CHECKPOINT: WHAT WOULD YOU DO?

Your friend Alley is sad because someone may be bullying her. She tells you about it instead of an adult because she is too shy and embarrassed. What could you do to help her?

GLOSSARY

bullying (BU·lee·ing): Repeated behavior intending to hurt, scare, or embarrass one or more people

cycle of bullying (SAI·kl uhv BU·lee·ing): A series of events that leads someone who was bullied to become a bully themselves

kindness (KINED·nes): Being considerate of others

pattern (PA·tern): Something that is repeated

power (PAU·ur): Having influence over others

provoke (pruh·VOKE): To incite or stir up

purpose (PUR·puhs): In a way that is intended or planned

school counselor (skool KOWN·se·ler): An adult at school you can go to when you need help

unkind (uhn·KINED): Unfriendly or unpleasant

upstander (UHP·stan·der): A person who does something to interrupt someone being bullied

INDEX

WEBSITES TO VISIT

www.dosomething.org/us/causes/bullying

https://www.stopbullying.gov/prevention/bystanders-to-bullying

www.aacap.org/AACAP/Families_and_Youth/Resource_Centers/Bullying_Resource_Center/Home.aspx

ABOUT THE AUTHOR

Vicky Bureau was born in Longueuil, Quebec, and was raised in South Florida. As a teacher, she developed a passion for the social and emotional growth of her students and later transitioned into the area of child and adolescent psychology after earning her master's degree in school counseling. In addition to working with children, Vicky loves to be surrounded by animals and nature. She lives in Fort Lauderdale with her family: Billy, Khloe, M.J., and Max; her three cats, Alley, Baguette, and Salem; and her dog, Boomer.

Written by: Vicky Bureau
Cover designed by: Rhea Magaro Wallace
Interior designed by: Kathy Walsh
Series Development: James Earley
Proofreader: Kathy Middleton
Educational Consultant: Marie Lemke M.Ed.

Photographs: Shutterstock Cover robert_s, Viktoriia Protsak, Brocreative; Background robert_s; Color Splash Viktoriia Protsak, Box p 5, 9, 15, 24, 28 Puwadol Jaturawutthichai; p 4 Marish; p 5 Monkey Business Images; p 6 Marish; p 7 Motortion Films; p 9 YanLev; p 10 gpointstudio, Jason Richeux; p 11 Pressmaster; p 13 Brocreative; p 15 CMotortion Films; p 17 Rawpixel.com; p 19 Sweet Memento Photography; p 20 Dmytro Zinkevych; p 21 Africa Studio; p 22 wavebreakmedia; p 24 VH-studio; p 26 Motortion Films; p 28 Motortion; p 29 Daniel Hoz

---

Crabtree Publishing

crabtreebooks.com 800-387-7650

Printed in the U.S.A./012023/CG20220815

Published in Canada
Crabtree Publishing
616 Welland Ave.
St. Catharines, Ontario
L2M 5V6

Published in the United States
Crabtree Publishing
347 Fifth Ave
Suite 1402-145
New York, NY 10016

Library and Archives Canada Cataloguing in Publication
Available at Library and Archives Canada

Library of Congress Cataloging-in-Publication Data
Available at the Library of Congress

Hardcover: 978-1-0396-6046-5
Paperback: 978-1-0396-6241-4
Ebook (pdf): 978-1-0396-7037-2
Epub: 978-1-0396-7235-2